Jean-Pierre Makosso
Muane Ma M'kayi
Hun'tchimbukune buendi Koku

Human works

Told by
MA M'KAYI

Éditions Dédicaces

HUMAN WORKS, *by Jean-Pierre Makosso*

Photo : JOANNA MACKENZIE ENGA
Translated from French to English by MICHEL POATI-TCHICAYA

Dépôt légal :
Bibliothèque et Archives Canada
Bibliothèque et Archives nationales du Québec

Un exemplaire de cet ouvrage a été remis
à la Bibliothèque d'Alexandrie, en Egypte

ÉDITIONS DÉDICACES INC
6285, rue De Jumonville
Montréal (Québec) H1M 1R7
Canada

www.dedicaces.ca | www.dedicaces.info
Courriel : info@dedicaces.ca

© Copyright - tous droits réservés – Éditions Dédicaces inc.
Toute reproduction, distribution et vente interdites
sans autorisation de l'auteur et de l'éditeur.

Jean-Pierre Makosso

Human works

Acknowledgements

It was during a school tour in Saskatchewan that most poems in this collection were written. I am sincerely grateful for the hospitality experienced in the province of Saskatchewan. Throughout my texts, I took time to affix to the end of each poem the city in which I was staying at the time, a personal way to express my sincere gratitude.

I thank the cities of Ottawa, Montreal, and I want to especially stress how the 32nd book fair in Sherbrooke was of particular interest, giving me the opportunity to visit another part of Canada, this great country.

I want to thank Marc, a schoolboy of nine years old from Saskatchewan who told me a story he learned from his father:

"My father told me:
A very long time ago
White people – just like us – went to Africa
They destroyed everything; they chased you around
You ran away everywhere because
You, black people, did not want to be their slaves.
Is this true?"

He was a great inspiration to me in achieving this work. To this young, sensitive and mature soul, I dedicate this work with all my heart.

Big thanks to Naolicha Ly Maxy my daughter to whom I asked to think about an introductory text that would link well with these *"HUMAN WORKS."* From Tunis where she resides for her university studies, she sent me *The Dying One*, which I have therefore attached at the end of the book.
In The *Dying One, one* discovers the way all African dictators die. I will not mention their names here because the list would be endless. They fight against their death and the welfare of their neighbours for decades, and then one day they fall in, suffering from the cancer of power. Paralyzed, they can't even chase a mouse gnawing at their feet or a mosquito buzzing in their ears or stinging their cheeks. Africans

are rooted in solidarity otherwise they would all become the prey of flies.

Thank you Maxy for that poem about these walking and dying individuals, ignorant of their fate and their own state. They all end up dying before the age of the illustrious *Nelson Mandela*. If they could be as good a democrat as he has been, they would live longer and remain active, while awaiting a glorious death.

Thanks to you who just bought the book. I suggest that you not read this book as a simple novel or a collection of poems. This is a story of genuine past events. It is a true story experienced by women then told by Ma M'kayi to her daughter *NANDJI* around the fire.
It is a poetic story that is to be read – or better – told, or narrated from the first to the last page, that is to say from the Orphans to The Dying One.

Thanks to each one of you who has been in my path and to you also dear friend who has given me a loaf of bread and served me a glass of water while away from home and from Ma M'kayi I was hungry and thirsty.

MUANE MA M'KAYI
(Ma M'kayi's child)

« I am a griot[1] from a long line of wise masters of eloquence. We are the book of mankind. Listen to my story you who think you know and you will know what you do not know. »

Give instruction to a wise man, and he will be still wiser
Teach a righteous man, and he will increase his learning.
Proverb 9:9

---

[1] Traditional storyteller

Introduction

Human Works is the latest book by Jean-Pierre Makosso. Indeed, Jean-Pierre Makosso submits a set of views and assessments on current society, a theme so dear to him. This time he does not hesitate to let a woman talk, Ma M'kayi, that storyteller of his childhood, also his own mother, and whose stories are constantly replaying in his head, prompting him to express that mood on stage and through writing.

Through his mother, who is most valuable and so dear to him in this world, Jean-Pierre Makosso exposes an unwavering point of view, an intense watch on a society that lives for appearances, in ignorance and indifference. The author withholds himself and gets strengthened by the woman who appears to be his dove, his pillar, his rock and his safe shelter. He legitimises his views, his demands and his anger at the social drift that continues to destroy but also tries to make his humble contribution: a real and universal awareness beyond simple words that flatter and entice.

As a man of dialogue and performance, the author has a commitment to build, inform, reassure and entertain, not only children (*the emerging force of the future of mankind*) as he always calls them but also the adults who surround these youngsters.
His shows are an open dialogue of outspokenness that whisper to the heart of every sheep in us. Some goats are obviously unrecoverable.
The author is neither a saviour nor a traitor, but just a human like you and me. He has something to say. Now he does it with all his heart!
In his usual simple and direct style, sometimes raw and funny as it is in the open dialogue of a storyteller or singer, the author takes the reader into meditation, universal awareness and encouragement to learn how to see past one's nose, rather than gaze at one's navel.

MICHEL POATI-TCHICAYA

Poetry is so difficult to write
Almost impossible to read
And not so easy to follow
We must therefore live it
So that the poet is proud
To have chosen for you such beautiful verses

JEAN-PIERRE MAKOSSO

To Joanie Thompson, Anatole Collinet, Elena Rogers
Who knew how to reach out
To those who were far away

To Martin Luther King
For whom the dream was reality
And as to live it, one should believe in it and not fight

To Nelson Mandela, Yvette B. Makosso
That loyalty, patience and courage
Ranked among the wise ones

To Barack Obama, Maxy Manon Makosso
The ones who have but an ideal, a goal
Believing they could while remaining positive

To Abraham Lincoln
Who got no threats or blackmail
But through and thanks to wisdom did abolish slavery

To you black slaves, colonized, martyrs of the independence
Victims of dictators
Our freedom is at the end of your sufferings and your sorrows
You are our heroes

To Prisca Foutou Tati, to orphans, to children and especially to all of you who adopt
Them worldwide
May they through you run freely and laugh
With the sparrows

*The book should be appreciated as a whole,
only afterwards will a terrible morality emerge.*

BAUDELAIRE

Preface

Poetry often comes from the imagination but also the heightened perception of reality. It is this double sense that one can experience from reading this book by Jean-Pierre Makosso.

Of course major topics are frequently discussed, but never with pointless pathos. Instead, the poet turns his cries of outrage or his songs of anger into prayers, a calling for hope and brotherhood. Better, according to him, to let oneself go to humanism rather than being overwhelmed by despair, even within a context that could incite it.

Moreover, we find with great emotion that despair can be transformed simply by a request for help, leading instead to wonderful, limitless beliefs.

Who would not be discouraged, by experiencing destruction, or by seeing one's hope always crushed on the same wall? Instead, the poet shows us that sincere prayer is never in vain, that it always finds a base, on which to build. Thus:

God of heavens! Hardness, what a rock, you poor dust
Observe beautiful nature in peace
Be attentive to its prayer
Isn't this the peace that you would like?

In other words: can we not find at our own front door what we are not used to seeing because our eyes are blinded by our own despair, our suffering?

HUMAN WORKS are works of love, of peace, and which find in themselves their greatest strength: this is the message from Jean-Pierre Makosso that I now invite you to discover.

THIERRY ROLLET
writer, literary agent

Abraham came near the Lord and said: "Would you also destroy the righteous with the wicked? Suppose there were fifty righteous men within the city, would you also destroy the place and not spare it for the fifty righteous that were in it? Far be it from you to do such a thing as this, to slay the righteous with the wicked, so that the righteous should be as the wicked; far be it from you! Shall not the judge of all the earth do right?"
So the Lord said: "If I find in Sodom fifty, forty five, forty, thirty, twenty or ten righteous within the city, then I will spare the whole place for their sakes…
I will not destroy it on account of the ten."

(GENESIS 18: 23-32)

"Humanity only needs ten righteous persons therefore the world would not be destroyed… let's find them in each one of us"

BOOK ONE

Nobody knows which tree I burned to proceed for this plantation. Let us just consider its products.
Fana Soro, Ivoirian artist and balafonist

I will defend my opinions to the death, but I will give up my life for you to defend your own.
Baudelaire

The truth is an offence but not a sin.
Bob Marley

Let us accept it as such and therefore let us pray together:
"Father forgive us our offences
As we forgive those who sin against us,
And especially help us not to destroy this world
That you love so."

Orphans

I

The continent is very sad; one can silently listen
To the devouring flies with their buzzing.
They lovingly land on bodies
Riddled with bullets that children, still
Hopeful, do call in vain

Thus begins a life of orphans
The witness sky looks helplessly upon
The river flowing red with blood;
Smiling yet sad the sky regretfully
Imitates its reflection in the tide of blood.

II

And little weeping orphans
Blow gently in the ears of sleepers;
With their quivering voices in a golden timbre,
They feel abandoned to their fate.
In the sky still hang offensive bombers
Ready to execute the fatal and decisive action.
The heat is cold… once again as usual,
Man and war have struck again very hard
Cries and tears of mourning arise all around
And death as a widow waits at the doorstep.
Close by, mothers of the children
Undergo another experience, poor mommies!
In pain and mourning, humiliated and raped
They cry poor women, their faces veiled
With sadness, with tears of despair, what a treachery!

Sir, dear sir, accept my forgiveness
You who on the eve of your birth,
Was for me a great deliverance!
The maternal memory remains my pain
In the dry season; and the freshness

Of the morning made you open your eyes
As I raised mine towards God;
You were covered in blood, my blood
I took you in my arms you were innocent.

III

Your father, proud and great, was watching us
We were the flock that he jealously guarded.
He was alive next to you; you had a father
You were on my tummy; I was your mother
You were not exposed to danger.
With that radiant weather, no bad thoughts
Came across the humans' minds
Who lived piously as saints.
No man hunting; the political family
My God… was but a small herd of funny people
Who, day and night, were monitoring temperatures
Rain, sun, good weather, that nature,
Faithful friend to laughing and joyful children
Among them you, running here and there, happy!
You took rain showers and sunbaths
You fell asleep. A smile waited for your awakening…
Outside the cock was inviting you and immediately
You went towards it before its cock-a-doodle-doo!
You ran after it while it was always ahead,
Taking you away… far away from your parents.

IV

As free as the goat of Mr. Seguin[2]
In the open air, in the fresh air you were running towards your gain.
A glorious destiny opened to you so mildly,
In a world where there was neither lion nor wolf;
In the life of men and birds
You were the people's friend and that of the cattle.
The whole world was safe, so safe was the big world!
There was always a door wide open, almond-scented!

---

[2] Mr Seguin is a story from Alphonse Daudet's book (*Les lettres de Mon Moulin*) about
Mr Seguin's goat, which escaped from the manger and discovered for one day the
joy of the mountain and freedom, and that was the best moment of its life.

Safe for all as a child's dream
And that door opened towards adolescence...
You reached it freely towards a bright future
Behind it was a smile and a happy memory!
The songs of the nightingales filled with blessings
Spread from your way any curse.
Repeated breaths and murmurs were our wishes for happiness,
Distant wishes of relatives, lots of warmth!

Sorrowful veiled widows weep
While in their veins runs the blood of the devil...
They cry poor orphans
Under the sky, the only witness...

V

Children feel no hatred or vengeance
They know neither honour nor glory. Bad luck
Faithful throughout their journey,
Settles down wickedly, quietly among them.
Today they are their own parents; tomorrow
Their fate will be in their own hands.
No man no god will turn to them,
Unless the one created in God's image:
Man, the very man with a human heart
Not the religious, not the politician
Rather the poet, the righteous one, not the emotionless heart
But the man of love who is still alive on earth,
Pushes away from them starvation and disease
Civil wars and guns
Unless the woman, the righteous, the true one, faith-filled,
Even in her labour pains rises and cries out loud
"Enough!
Stop!"
While the drilled bodies still litter the earth...
And the echo commands the weapons to keep quiet
"Stop in the name of God!
Cease fire!"

VI

Then the brave children get up at last
Through an innocent glance defy the murderers
They advance towards them, wipe their tears.
Hypnotized the murderers drop their weapons.
Without a word children reach their tormentors
And through the two horns they hold the bulls.

The sky opens, wonders
Like a flower that awakens
For love
In daytime
Above it a fly silently
Intones another buzz
More joyous
Much happier

Ascension

Through the night sky full of stars I will fly high
Towards cottony peaks piercing the clouds.
Caught in drunkenness, outdoor in flight
I will reach the goal of my voyage.

I will ascend into infinity without a word
To no one but God will I raise my voice
In poetry, in song so that these evils
By my faith - and his power be gone from me.

Faith and hope

I

The sun, star of heat and fire
Pours its rays over the holy places
Where pious women on Good Friday
At noon fasting true to their destiny
Get up, bend over, and stand up
Curl, twist, prostrate
Then raise their hands as at the bar
And all together *'Allahhu akbar!'*

'God is Great' the prayer is arising

The moon, transparent plate without flame
Casts its soft light on Muslim women and their imam

Christian women on the eve of Christmas
At midnight put their vowels and consonants
Into sentences full of supplications
Hands raised up they anticipate justification

For them Jesus is just and the prayer is arising

The prayer touches the heart of spirits and ancestors
Leaving monks and priests indifferent
Who turn to God and point the finger
To dusty tablets of Moses and his law
Eye for an eye, tooth for a tooth
And the night falls on the setting sun
Like a hungry beast that pounces on its prey;
The man lowers his eyes and loses his faith
God so ashamed scolds the sky and tears
Of rain, fall on holders of weapons.

II

Please do not tell me about Joseph
Who was falsely accused by the wife of his chief.
He lived far from his childhood and his birthplace
Survived, thanks to the help of his God.
Read your holy book once more
He knew no dictatorship
Married in Egypt
He lived far from his homeland
A happy family life
Where butterflies came out of caterpillars
Kept on flying
Arising
High in the sky
Pious!

Open your Bible
Moses was targeted
Received the power from Heaven
Right from the throne of God
And though furious
Did die old

III

Misery, my pain is in my patience
Despair, my patience is in my suffering

O Misery! O Despair!
I regret that time of black Africa!

Bantu people imploring their gods with joy
Felt their big voices vibrating
Banging the walls of the rocky mountains
Where doubtful bats
Did sound their shrill cries
Thus raising animals with a snarl.
At a time when clouds were forming in the sky
Working bees were busy for honey
Which children would happily pick up the next day
By expressing joyful sighs!

IV

Belief! I do believe mother Africa
Exotic continent, your misery
Is the result of a man of the law
Who set an innocent man on the cross!
Mother earth
Sky sea
Africa
Exotic
Your cross I will bear
O faith, yes your cross I will raise it up by my faith
Because I soiled you, I stained you
I gave you as hostage; I imprisoned you
In the name of God and religion
On behalf of the spirits and tradition.
My anger, my great madness
Is nothing but stupidity… is it a value?
Death in heart I bear a pale face
Which I dare not wipe with dirty hands!

V

"On the run
And all after him
Horses, dogs
And all his friends
On donkeys, on camels
Run quickly and take his skin
Dead or alive, preferably alive!
Put him under arrest that traitor, that wanderer
So that he suffers the punishment
That of the children of the New Testament
Who by us were beheaded one after another
When we went in search of the holy child."

-Yes, quietly they exterminated
The newborn ones, the children; they accomplished
The order of man and his madness
Who believes he is God and that there is but him
The only king, the leader in heaven, on land, and sea
The one and only master of the universe!

May the woman mourn! Ignore the pain
That rises in her and burns her breast!
The world is thirsty; pollute water
Let the herd die.
From the stick, from the gun make the blood flow!
Innocents bow and bend, all in a row
Walk, walk to the slaughterhouse
Turn off the light and all in darkness
Fire!
Place your bets!
Game of death at gunpoint
Look without frowning your eyebrows
And when the evening comes switch off, no light.
With gratitude recite your prayers
Thank the one up there, the Lord
For he does give you an everlasting life.

VI

Who will know it, history does forget
It can't be told any longer, the man denies it
He flees far from his destiny to another
Shameful one, which he enjoys to its fullest way
We will know nothing; ignorance
Is the evil of our suffering!
Our only reason for living is to mature
Mature without dying but nourishing

"Gather our bones and skeletons
Make labels of them
A great export, isn't it?
Swap them with nuclear bombs in the name of the nation!"

With open sky, closed heart
And nature ceases to exist
A song, a voice without melody rises
From the horizon, spreads around the world;
With open sky, searches closed hearts
And warns the world of the danger.
Danger of dying is the affliction to death
Fear of death is the danger resulting in death
Death that leaves me to my own fate
Fate that leaves me in the cold of death!

VII

O rocky mountain, O Royal Mountain!
A song of love, O tropical song!
The sky closes on the receding horizon
Plain and sky to it they join
The horizon is trapped like a grain of sand
As captive as a child listening to a fable!
Between two teeth crushed the captive horizon
And the child in the fable, harmless
Searching for himself, lost, discovers himself.
There at the horizon the sky opens
To the wind, to the air, to space, free!
Freedom finds its strengths, vibrates,
Twists, stretches, lengthens, rages
And gradually doubles its strengths, drags
Towards the grain of sand between two teeth
Draws from the abyss the poor child.
The child arrives, takes his role
In front of the man, that funny one
Who tries to show off
Who plays the devil

-There's always someone smarter than you!

The child looks up, laughs
Black laughs with white teeth
Milk teeth, frank teeth
Hidden by black lips…taciturn
Thick lips with night laughter
Laughter rises proudly
In a noisy tone which makes pulsate
Princesses and Queens and their pretty smiles
Turn happily to the future.
In the horizon arise songs of praise
Honouring children as angels!

Mutual transition

I

In the final ray of the setting sun
Summer has gently finished its term
One can still hear the joyous laugh of children
On the beach, in the mountains, in the forest during that season!

Birds in trees sing the anthem
"Good bye sunny season and see you later."
The transition takes place peacefully, here the fall!
Unlike the man who in war goes on training

In order to establish and dominate he divides, he reigns, he judges
Refuses to follow Nature and its course.
As a dictator king he keeps the seat
And mercilessly bombs all around

The trees are shedding their leaves
Ready to receive the new Queen.
Flowers on the threshold bow down
And the fall rises to the stage.

II

How beautiful this transition of seasons is!
All follow the normal course of things
Summer autumn winter and spring
Each returning after a short break

The leaf falls but never revolts
The bear considers the cold with patience
Waiting without complaint the time of harvest
In this natural quiet man loses his conscience

His heart refuses to listen to the song of nature
He closes his eyes to the constitution
Over beauty of nature he chooses torture
He blocks his ear to the songs of birds and persists in rebellion

"God of heavens! Hardness, what a rock, you poor dust
Watch beautiful nature in peace
Be attentive to its prayer
Isn't this the peace that you would like?"

Smile and memory

Let the child live
Live freely and grow
Let the mom smile
Live free and smile

Under her smile kindly hides
Her pretty laugh
Which reveals tenderly
A beautiful memory

She gave him life with a big smile
With great joy she saw him grow
The time of his birth is her greatest memory
She will never bear that of his death

Let the child live
Live grow live
Let the mom smile
Laugh live smile

Homeless

To the black child a white coat
Cry, cry the orphans
Orphans of white sand
The skeleton of the dolphin

The hand, the hand presenting its back
Its little fingers gesticulating skyward
And clicking into a nice set
Invite, invite the hand to a duel

Fingers intertwine between them shouting at each other
Like black witches with night eyes
Who once had big mouths!
Look the time is running away!

There, orphans with stomachs aching
We can ignore them they are among us
Consider hunger as a dance but now
They are gesticulating; can you see them?

O funny human the cry that is rising
Almost every day and which clings to your skin
Wouldn't it be nice if you took it away
From the child instead of turning your back ?

The mother hen leads her chicks
Scratching a grain here and there, bravo!
So are they looking for the feast!
Wheat, rice and corn for all, it's beautiful!

The wind blows to the great dance of the trees, woe!
The sky roars like a raging hyena
Each animal goes to his home
The rain falls. Where do these lost orphans go?

Come on let us help these innocent and homeless ones
Who are running without knowing where to turn
One prayer on their almost lifeless lips:
'Oh God oh God, why have you forsaken us?'

Come on let us rescue them in the name of humanity
If not let us applaud as it is a mere comedy
To see these children being swept away
In such a tragedy

The hand makes little fingers squirt
The little fingers are giggling and teasing her.
Orphans far away from the abyss leave without a voice.
Above the abyss soar swallows

To the black child a white coat
Sing, sing orphans
Orphans of white sand
The skeleton of the dolphin

BOOK II

We must learn to live together as brothers or perish together as fools
Martin Luther King

Nandji or she

Nandji, walking, walking, her black feet in love on
The white sand; happy beautiful girl
Almost a child! She sees boats coming. She's so pure
So sweet! She counts her naked footsteps to the lovely sea

"Where are these boats from," the beautiful girl wonders
"I'd love to know from where these big machines come!"
Then another day boats depart away from her.
"Where are they going so early this morning?"

"So where do these large freights go?
One day I'd like to go where these large ships go!"
Then Nandji performs a merry dance on the beach.

The boats push the white foam on the shore
Nandji takes some in her hand
Drinks it and gets drunk with joy as after a drop of wine

Nandji Iya Navandji or she and the other

Another day at the beach Nandji, running, running
Drunk with happiness, joyous, laughing
Her black feet bare on the white sand
She sees other humans coming, white families
Among them Navandji, a girl of her age
That she looks right in the face.
Navandji looks away shy
Nandji moves her humid hands towards Navandji
She wants to touch her but Navandji seized with fear
Runs to hide behind a flower
Of the sea which opens
On that calm and silent morning in July
"Where are these people from, and we look alike
I would like to know where they come from?"
Unfortunately Nandji and Navandji do not speak the same language
She is willing to talk to the other but in vain
Then she begins to dance slowly at the edge of the sea
And Navandji comes slowly hiding behind her mother
She sings a song in *Vili* dialect inviting the other to come
Navandji reveals herself little by little giving Nandji a weak smile
Then approaching her touches her skin
And with her athletic legs runs to the water;
Without waiting Nandji follows her
Glad to have found a new friend.
Alas, comes the evening, time to say goodbye
They agree to meet in the same place
Navandji leaves accompanied by her parents
White families
Nandji sees them climb into the great liner
"Where do all these people go with their rucksacks?"
She sees them disappear behind the sea
She runs and asks her mother
"Mom what is there beyond the horizon?

Do people live there whom we do not know?"
"There, her mother says, is where waves are formed
There, that's where all the jokes are told."
Eager for jokes Nandji wants to go
There, in the land of waves never to return.
Maybe there she would see her friend again
The other; sure Navandji is anxious to see her too
Unless she has already forgotten about her
No you never forget someone you have loved.

In the dark night Nandji goes to the beach
Ready to face the sea swimming
Behind her the fire is crackling and her mother is calling
Nandji turns back and sees sparks
Surrounding the fire, ready for the story of the night.
She will listen to the tale then she will leave at midnight.

The tale of Ma M'kayi [3]

A poor man slowly plodding his way
An ostrich egg his only loot.
On his way he met a banana planter
Whose only belonging was a climbing rope
He swapped it with the egg because he was hungry,
And the man willingly parted with his booty
Took the climbing rope and left the planter.
The egg boiling in the pot let out a steam.
The man on his way met a *malafoutier*[4]
Under the palms and wondering how to get to the top of the tree.
"Take my climbing rope if you want, said the man
I'll come later to take it back."
"Good!" The *malafoutier* went on collecting palm wine.
Happy with his gain he calmly climbed down.
At the foot of the palm tree the rope broke in two.
At the same time the man came back joyfully
"Give back my rope, my climbing rope
Was given to me by the banana planter
The banana planter was hungry
I gave him the egg I had, my only loot."
The *malafoutier* gave him wine
And the man went on his way rejoicing.
Later he met hunters who were eating meat.
They were thirsty, and he offered them palm wine
As lemonade, advising them not to drink it all
Because he would also be thirsty by the evening time.
The meat eaters did not take this into account

---

[3] Ma M'kayi is a famous storyteller of the Tchimpoko family in the Vili tribe. Refer to The voice of the storyteller by the same author.
[4] Malafoutier: The malafoutier is the one who climbs up palm trees with a climbing rope made of African wild creeper to extract and collect palm wine.

They quenched their thirst by emptying the entire bottle
"Give me my wine given to me by the *malafoutier*
The *malafoutier* broke my climbing rope
A rope I got from the banana planter who took my loot
An egg which I had while I was on my way."
The hunters gave him a goatskin
He put it under his armpit and ran like a hare
Just before the crossroads he met lumberjacks
Who asked him if a lion was chasing him
No, he said. He was in a hurry and wanted to arrive early
"You have there a beautiful skin," said the lumberjacks
"Take half of it". – "Thanks! You are a very nice lad."
They used all the skin to make their tom-toms
"My skin, he angrily said, hunters' skin who drank the *malafoutier's* wine
This clumsy lad who broke my climbing rope
Rope of the banana grower who took my booty
The only booty that I had when I set on my way."
The lumberjacks gave him a drum
That he began playing, keeping the vultures away.
At dusk he reached the next village, dark without light
Teenagers were dancing the *lelikage*[5]
He stayed still watching them his drum on his shoulder
They played music by tapping on sheet metal
He lent them his tom-tom, which they drummed till morning
Then the skin burst and the dance party ended
"My drum," he cried, "wealth from lumberjacks these brothers

---

[5] The lelikage or hanging is a dancing style by youngsters from the Vili tribe. Refer to the poem entitled "la pendaison" in Le cri du triangle by the same author.

Who took my fair skin, my beautiful goatskin
Given to me by hunters
Those meat eaters and smooth talkers
Who drank the sweet wine of the *malafoutier*
That clumsy lad who broke my climbing rope
While coming down the palm tree
A rope that was given to me by the banana planter
To whom I gave my only loot
An ostrich egg I had while on my way."
The chief gave him a teenager to whom he got married
Heart full of joy he took her in his village
And there in his village the teenager became pregnant
She wore the costume of woman and ceased to be a saint
Later she embraced the role of mother and had a daughter
A girl who grew up alongside her, beautiful and very nice

- That girl handed to be married - was it you, mother?
And the man with the ostrich egg - where is he? Is he my father?
- No Nandji, they are your great, great, great-grandparents
To understand everything we have to go back to the dawn of time.

BOOK III

Literature is set to walk into the future by remembering the past
(Jean D'Ormesson of the French Academy)

« *I am a griot from a long line of wise masters of the verb.*
From Mame Gnigni, Kaliste, Loufoule, Monique Pambou, Tchissimbu Loufonshine, Toukoule tû mâtine, Ngouale Longuile, Tâ N'gudi loembh, Bob Bilèle, Nombu Situ Paule and herself
MAM'KAYI
We are the History of Humanity
Listen to our legend so you will know what you do not know.»

The history

We lived in family and community
Among trees that had delicious fruits
Animals were jealous of our peace and freedom
They applied the policy of the strongest one, and slaughtered themselves.

Men were a strong safety barrier
Protecting the village against the ferocious ones
Women felt safe,
Behind each of them hid a force

Force of good and not of evil
Which seemed perfectly normal
Because we had respect for our customs and way of living

We knew our values and our rights
We observed our traditions and our laws
In peace, and tranquillity without bitterness

Abundance

There was a deafening noise
We saw something gigantic
The sea heaved a strange roar

It was prior history, after history or the flawless history
The age of chipped stone
Our houses made of mixed mud and grass, roofs covered with straw
Protected us against all odds

Hunting, breeding, fishing, gathering
Activities and professional life
Kept us from all sorts of debts
Because we lived a life of traditional trade

No matter what was happening elsewhere
We were not informed but we were not ignorant.
In our corner of the earth we were the best.
We studied plants; we were people of wisdom.

We had fire, we had wool, and we had water
We had our languages, our religions and a great culture
We grew coffee, cotton and cocoa
All around us lay beautiful and green nature

We had oil but we preferred wood
We had pure air, the moon, the stars, the sun and its beautiful sunsets.
We did not have presidential elections. We had good kings
Who made sure that everything was fine before going to bed.

We had gold, diamonds, nothing but precious stones,
We had cowry shells, which in our view were worthier
We did not expect better than a peaceful and happy life.
Death was a natural transition to another life without pain.

There was music, song and dance
What else? Oh yes! Life was crazy with laughter
When they were together there was always a great mood around
That made us live in paradise, oh what to say!

I'm not saying anything else just watching still.
How to explain it! The sea was roaring that day
The wind whistled violently… so strong
And the waves rose from the horizon

There was a deafening noise
We saw something gigantic
The sea heaved a grotesque roar

Stampede

It was a stampede, racing, running away
They were attacking strong and robust men
The manhunt, the chasing
Through forest, creepers, bush, and dead leaves

Stampede into the unknown
Feet, hands and the head were running
Everywhere barking, voices, orders: "Where are you going?
This way, that way," as directed to the barking dog

Our butts bitten by the fangs of the beast left a taste
Of pain and especially
Of great suffering

A blow to the head, our men fell and immediately their hands tied
And their feet bound
They were already seeking deliverance

The black king and the white master
or
The Wicked and the Tyrant

He was seated
Under the shade of the large tree
Black king, in front of him
White master, marbled still

He the king, seated on his chair
Of black ebony wood
Felt at ease.
His feet shivering on a woollen cloth

Around him young and beautiful maidens
Gently massaged his shoulders
With their soft and lovely hands.
The king was smiling like a clown

The white master, pink like a pig
In front of these maids bare and firm breasted
Was feeling the sweat on his skin.
He roused himself without embarrassment to the exciting view

Far away they were taken
Our brave and valiant hunters
In an iron monster that was humming;
King and master laughing at our sorrow

Our lips were quivering – A breath – 'No!'
Our watery eyes – A hand gesture – 'Farewell!'
We were abusively swearing: 'Damn, you devils!'
And to heaven: 'We who believed you were the righteous God!'

"Well! We have two words to say to you
Yes, just two words: be blessed!
Since you do not want to bless us
Then tell us: " Why are we being punished?"

He was seated
Under the shade of the large tree
The wicked king, in front of him
The white tyrant, marbled still

The white master

The master:

"Look, this is our covenant
Yes, our contract
Accepted, signed without resistance
Hand in hand, and then cheers!"

The king did not understand a word, not at all
At sunset
He shook hands with the white master…oh no!
They were alike

Yeah right, my foot, that's what he thought
Poor black man!
The master with his crooked smile
You had to see it!

He laughed at this indigenous one
In this enclave;
He wanted to quickly leave the village
And take away his slaves.

One last glass of champagne
Then a nice hug
Of accomplice-enemies in the countryside
No more fun

"Rifles, liquor and all the poison
Take it all
Men, gold, diamonds and even the zircon
Give them to us!"

Slaves because of the greedy king
Macaques, savages
Vocabulary of the devil master
Became our names on this beach

The wicked black king with his head
Merrily
Nodded with such a stupid laugh
To the mad slave dealer

The black king

The king:

"Here we have a pact
A pact in blood
Together let us produce good acts
To satisfy the white man."

We understood nothing, absolutely nothing
What was the king saying?
Was this the way one spoke to one's family?
Well, what a funny voice!

Then a strong breeze arose
Moved us
Slowly as dead leaves
Then kissed us.

The breeze whispered in our ears
"The king is mad."
He, the king, as if waking from a bad sleep
Shouted: "On your knees!"

Execution! And his guards our blood brothers
Without hesitation
To satisfy the desires of the wicked and that of the tyrant
In a rush

Burst in - in spite of their will
Sticks raised
On those who were for many
Protectors and elders

Our forests smelled of blood and sap.
The animals
Were watching us. Was it a dream?
"Black people, they said, what a bad flock!"

Sale

This was the era of slavery!
The black king corrupted
No longer fed himself of livestock
But of the…

Trafficking of men. The sale of macaques
Who were violently beaten
By soldiers; with truncheon blows
They beat them brutally.

They were executing the order of the wicked king
That traitor
He who was executing the order of the tyrant master,
That crazy

A different history from ours
Was written
A blank page the other ones
Were soiling

With red blood and
Salty tears
Innocent blood flowing through the gun
Of that scatterbrained master

Draining Africa of all human life
All Africans over there
Attached to chains
Advanced barely at walking pace.

Although they lost their roots,
Poor men!
They did not forget their origins,
Ours

Buzzed by a sea that roars
Poetic wave
Circling around
Bad political joke

Black king, white boss, comfortably at ease
In the shadow of the fields
Attended the macaques being cooked over the coals
As if by magic

How horrible things were
At that time
How terrible the moments were
And although

Already gone those buried
Memories
Still run into the future
That is fleeing!

There, where waves are formed
It is quite far
Where jokes are told
Do not go Nandji, come back!

BOOK IV

The most independent of all men is the one who said no to slavery
Francine Minville, The Evil in its Divinity

I'd rather be a free man in my grave than living as a puppet or a slave
Jimmy Cliff

Mission and vision

Later there were missionaries
Who looked more like visionaries
Their word in mind

Word of God - not that of the ancestors
Word of the priests
Not so stupid

We welcomed them
They were welcome
Abuse of trust

They looked at us differently
For them we were different
Funny mistrust

They lived in a house not in a cage
That was more comfortable than a hut
Beautiful colour

They felt so good living
Nature lovers they lived freely
Under the heat

Their feet covered with sandals
Were for us a scandal
For bare feet

We ran here and there, everywhere
In water, on hot sun or in mud
Unrestrained

That life was ours
We lived it thrilled
Under our raffia

Their sight with blue eyes
On our bodies of sun and fire
Followed our steps

Always proud and while praying
They were more interested in our land
Than in our food!
They were willing to sacrifice their holy book
For us to be drunk
From their scriptures

Foreigners I

Then there were sellers, buyers, hunters and masters of slavery
Kings and missionaries
Who always met at our beaches
To celebrate their anniversary!

The sacred book

I

We learned the Scriptures by heart
Every time we remembered the Ten Commandments
We were overwhelmed by a fear.
Our breath of life was the New Testament

It talked about the baby Jesus and his birth
His sacrifice, his forgiveness, and his grace;
In our conscience we were not guilty
The slave master was the one who opened the hunting

II

The missionary called us thieves. Not fair
Our theft was nothing but a lump of sugar, that's all
He stole diamonds, gold, and ivory. Very unfair
"You'll be sent to hell," he growled. "The blazing fire awaits you"

"Awful sinners, awful sinners, awful and dirty fishermen!"
He shouted constantly throughout the day.
What harm was there in being a fisherman?
Dirty we were, certainly yes, particularly while fishing

III

Many abandoned their nets to follow him.
According to him every fisherman was a sinner like Simon Peter
Nonsense what he was saying, one has to survive
He got rich by taking advantage of our lands

He was feeding us with these beautiful words
For he said: "Man is not fed with bread alone!"
At the end we were fed up with it
Our hungry bellies started moaning.

His words were not producing any miracle
Unlike those of the Christ they were without effect
Empty words without oracle
We had had enough

Foreigners II

Yes there were masters of slavery
 White bosses, black kings, and visionaries
Who always met on our shores
To celebrate; real bloodthirsty people

Slave hunters were there to serve
Sellers and buyers to haggle
Missionaries to curse and bless
The white boss and the black king to order

There was nothing else to do
All liars
And one had to watch them and keep quiet
Real criminals
Execute orders to satisfy
These great thieves
And put ourselves in prayer
While keeping our honour

Hell and Heaven

While they were emptying and looting our land
We were praying to God the father and his son
Believing in heaven, living hell.
"Close your eyes so that I may bless you"

Sang the missionary who had no power.
And we did close them to receive the curse
Amen! He is a god who laughs at our woes.
O nature, what a wicked seduction!

He is a god, a god without mercy.
The judgement, the thunder, the lightning, hell,
And then the man and his wealth auctioned

There is a God, a God of truth
Sacrifice, grace, forgiveness, salvation, heaven
One must believe and hope. And so life is!

Preaching

So stupid so black
"Close your eyes so that I can abuse you.
The present life is a life full of stories
Believe in the future life, the one I give you!"

So stupid so black
"Do not be interested in material goods
Believe in heaven and even without seeing it
It is here, turn to spiritual things."

Mulizine li Zambi![6] We believed him,
Joy to the heart and wordless lips
And he peered at us through his glasses

On behalf of the Lord we should not have listened.
But how to resist such an angel
He alone impersonated all the lies

---

[6] Mulizine li Zambi means: "In the name of God"

Baptism

In the dry season we had all swallowed
His gods, his demons, his prayers
We could not escape
From his deserted path

In the rainy season we vomited everything:
Our traditions, our culture, and our well being
To embrace what was neither
Our values nor our spirits nor our ancestors

Our sun was laughing
A yellow imperfect laugh…
Disowning our customs

And stars were dimming in a cloudless sky
Painting a sad landscape.
We had neglected the wisdom of the moon!

Currency of Judas

We forgot the song of the river
Madly clinging to the words of the fool.
Neither the sun nor the moon nor the stars were proud of us
And the morning fog warned us of the danger

Our fetish items lost their mystery;
Ancestral sacrifices were forbidden;
The missionary banned initiation rites
These he decried as sacrilege during his service

Religious service focused on Sunday charity.
The black king himself, his tongue in his pocket
Was merely contented with crumbs

Crumbs that the missionary offered him every night
When they came to meet in the corridor
After emptying his offering dish.

BOOK V

Do not imitate anyone or anything. A lion that imitates a lion becomes a monkey
Victor Hugo

The black king in white boots

The king lost his traditional costume
He turned into a masked clown
And offered a cultural show
A booted king in large jacket and white boots

Now he needed a table.
Not wanting to eat on the floor
Which he considered horrible
He preferred to have his own bowl.

The king's table, the king's plate, the king's fork.
"This is mine, this is for the king, and that is mine"
Was his new language

As for us - one foot to the missionary, one foot to the king
An iron fist, a wooden hand
It was all blackmail.

The new chief

Yes sir, yes sir, yes sir
Could be heard throughout the village
And one could swear on that god of heaven
Who attracted us all with his sweet statements.

He went from hut to hut early in the morning
Awakening men, greeting women, blessing children
He was god, he was pure, and he was a saint.
In his presence one was required to bow down: *"hello commander!"*

The royal praises were then sent to him
He became the new and respected leader so admired
And he relished every moment deliciously.

Our king so black so stupid became a grinning monkey-king.
Lands, forests, and all the space
Became private property. What an era!

A king's act

Where were we? Where were we going?
In the middle the white chief in a glorious position
White and steep, making good progress, so crazy
Jubilant, happy he saw through rose coloured glasses.

Beside him the black king was taking a nap.
After having drunk liquor and wine
Relieved himself in his pants, what an act!
And the white chief raised his evil laugh.

"To me this land, to me these seas, to me these skies
Burn your taboos, your fetishes and your gods,
 North, South, East, West, all is mine."

Flies hovered around the king
Who was adapting to his new life without choice.
He lost everything that was his.

The big speech

Then one day there was a big party. Under the shade
Of a large baobab tree the white chief was talking to people
We saw for the first time. Dark statements
Made of unknown words and quite engaging.

He spoke of colonization and colonizers
Designating us as these savages, former slaves, puppets.
Laughter rang out in the crowd, white and mocking laughs.
Around the black king flies buzzed a melody.

One page was being closed
Another one was quietly to be opened
There in front of the king and his smells.

One came out of the past, burning rags
In laughter, in humiliation, in slowness!
Griffins were carefully painted.

Death of the king

At the end of the speech we left, exhausted.
The king was stiff like a sculpture
Dead! Oh my! Had we been dreaming?
The future belonged to God, the Scriptures asserted.

Were we all trapped in a dream,
Whites, Blacks all within the same race,
In pursuit of a brief illusion,
Or were we looking for the happiness of all

Were we all fantastic shadows,
Blacks, Whites, stretched like rubber bands,
Our hands and our feet to celebrate All Saints

Or were we plunged into a deep sleep
On the evening of November 1st when the wake
Of the dead ones reminded us they all were saints

With no reply

"Lord, when the road is long
When in the distant horizon
We can see a thousand and one ways
Spare us doubt
And let us take the path of your choice
The one that for our people will be the good way!

Colonizers with deadly venom
Your bad breath pollutes the air
Waive your excess anger
Make your brains work
Repent if not fear Nature
She will hold you responsible I am sure

Everywhere on the black continent
Millions of ancestors sleep peacefully
Resting from their hard work in the fields
It is our duty to take care of their rest
Please do not come to change the established order
Go away! Please leave the place we are united

Lord, let them leave and go back where they came from
Their presence here is not your will
Thou shall not murder, thou shall not steal' is your word of truth
Saints in heaven release us from their bondage!"
This was our prayer to God
Wondering whether he was still in heaven.

BOOK VI

Our destiny is not written for us but by us
Barack Obama

...Then let us write another one, better for our children.
Maxy Manon

The colonized ones

I

Black-skinned, eyes surrounded by sleep
Knees bent in the name of God, his Son and the Holy Spirit
Emptiness! Our fingers clenched we anticipated his awakening.
Was he colonized too or was he busy?

Black-hearted, they made us work hard
In mines, in factories, in the fields, in their homes
From their seats they controlled our future
Which lay before them like a used book

II

The colonizers placed their seats
Under blazing sun that pierced our skin;
Having fled their homes of cold and snow
They came to dwell in ours like croaking toads

They controlled our kings and our warriors; they had nerve!
Even children in our wombs and on our breasts
Were monitored by them
Listed, numbered like grains

As for us while kneeling devout psalmist
Hands and fingers on the floor tapping it like a drum
Chanted in vain our sad prayers
Complaints and meditations of love

The wave broke down, stampede. The shipwreck
They arose from anywhere, real tabby cats
With rage in their heart.
What had we done to them, poor trash?

They thundered. The sweat ran down their bald heads
Wrongly or rightly! Wrongly!
Wrongly their eyes of wild beasts
Gleamed like gold nuggets

Their whips ready to scrape
Our backs held at the tip a deadly black poison
Which threw us on the ground and left us there, paralyzed
Sunk in a deep sleep until evening.

III

Waking up we felt empty, ignorant. Our tongues hanging out
Did the sun rise northward or westward?
Total confusion, our languages forgotten
The sun rose from the south and set in the east

The continent had been taken hostage
Another fate for another generation
From Africa to America slavery is over
The indigenous entered the school of colonization

X, Y, Z - learning the alphabet
Familiarizing himself with another culture, another message
New words and new letters - A, B
New teachers. Gone are the days of our wise ones!

Present! Absent!

In the meantime our surnames had been changed
In the meantime we bore their names;
First names that we received on the spot
Just because they could not spell our names:

Muane ma M'kayi Hun' tchimbukune
Muana Tosso Vuna Muaflambhe
Muissu munguku
Likoku buendi nkoku
Mâme n'zingue hubute n'bi
Ma m'kayi hubute n'botchi

In the meantime we had been forced to go to school
And when we heard our names we answered "present!"
In the meantime we had become school students. Very funny!
When we were not there others answered "absent!"

And the next day we were severely punished
For having missed a day of class
Our time of running free in the forest was over
We were no longer children of the hunting tribe.

Letters and numbers

We learned to read their letters
We learned to write their words
Warrior, war, soldier, sailor
And to count like good teachers

This was just too much knowledge
We had our letters, words and numbers; we could count
Raindrops in our language[7] and in happiness:
Moko, mibale, missato, mine, mitano

One, two, three, four, five
Playing, jumping, laughing
Running here and there, free, real children

Moko, mibale, missato, mine, mitano,[8] real kids
Sambanu, sambuadi, nana, hivua, kumi,[9] with our beautiful voices
Six, seven, eight, nine, ten, we referred to our ten fingers

---

[7] Linguala is the national language spoken in Congo-Brazzaville and Democratic Republic of Congo.
[8] Moko (one), mibale(two), missato(three), mine(four), mitano(five).
[9] Sambanu(six), sambuadi(seven), nana(eight), hivua(nine), kumi(ten).

False hope

We were sitting like submissive children in front of the dentist
Who played up and down with our teeth
He sank nails, pliers, scissors; a real chemist
He cut, pounded and blew. Stop, damn it!

Yet another trap, strange destiny
Tossed and burning alive, pain and burning
A sad heart in search of a feast
Good wine and good food

Then when he finished exploring our mouths with care
He set to the exploitation of our bodies
Collecting everything he needed.

He talked to us and drew us into a dream.
Desires distant hopes. Sleep!
A bitter taste of blood and sap!

BOOK VII

A law can never force a man to love me, but it is important that it prevents him from lynching me
Martin Luther King

Song of the griot

Then the song
Of the storyteller
Very high
Suddenly
Arose
In the valleys

Listen yes listen - you bloody vultures
Now above the green peaks
The black eagles go around.
They hold their wings wide open

They swoop down on your naked bodies
Spin faster; you have gold, diamonds, crude oil
What more are you looking for?
We accepted your schools.

Your music makes you crazy and us sick.
Listen to the sound of our tom- tom
So that it calms you
And heals your soul.

Here we are now, the eagles swoop down on these vultures
Their wings chase the air.
They glide; they are back
Furious and angry

Our heroes are coming
Out of your top universities
They come as the crow flies
They come to avenge the colonized people.

They have received your education and culture
They know the great law
They understand your paperwork
They are writing a new law

The law of equality
Independence
Freedom
In all conscience

Son of our ancestors born from slavery
Educated by your missionaries on our beaches
Colonized by your people in our village
Our intellectuals are landing. Leave our shores!

Independence (1960)

It was a bold stroke
Radiance
A knockout

Song: *'Independence cha cha to bakiri yeh!*
O lipanda cha cha to zuiyéh!'

People were singing across the continent
Lipanda! Independence!
The euphoria of the rising sun emerged
On all, great pleasures!

Moon and shooting stars
Herald
Ravishing news
Salvation

We kissed one another. Great time!
Like beautiful lovers
We held hands with no shock
Two by two

In the evening, just like children poets
We sang
Skylark! Nice skylark
And we composed

'Independence cha cha to bakiri yeh!'
All proud and all laughing
'O lipanda cha cha to zuiyeh!'
All black, all smiling

Yippee! They left our land. Shameful!
Tears and sadness
Time to say goodbye
Kindly

As bad lovers
They hated us
For these little painful moments
They cursed us

Poor nasty termites
Lack of gratitude
Old pots
Burning with ingratitude.

One man standing alone
Straight as an 'I'
Sang with us
"DO RE MI"

Only one man in front of the microphone
Coldly
Among all the procurators
Of people of his colour

Chanted with Africans
In Congo Brazzaville: "Free, free
Yes freedom is finally here
Free to live!"

It was a new birth
For all the indigenous;
We sang independence
On all our beaches

"Independence cha cha to bakiri yeh!"
Independence cha cha we won it, we got it!
"O lipanda cha cha to zui yeh!"
O independence cha cha, we have it!

BOOK VIII

When those in supreme power want to be relentlessly in first place, then let us pray that our path does not cross theirs.
Francine Minville, The Evil in his Divinity

The flag and the hat (1960-2010)

They dropped their flag
And behind them abandoned their hat

Was it a bold stroke?
Or just a feat
For it was not a knockout.

Poor us! It was like a wildfire that freedom.
Our Black Eagles were their black monkeys
Whom they fed with rotten bananas; shy and frightened
They swallowed all the orders of the whites. Real funnels!
And us, poor women, disgusted!

Africa was struggling while bound;
Some of our children even shivering
Were willing to fight to prevent this crisis,
Independence, new weapon for the white colonizers
Who already had grip on other black people

There were already those who by them were trained
In struggle, battle and weapons.
The settlers had all their names on paper
Names of corrupted black monkeys ready to raise the alarm
To betray their brothers, distorting their path.

They simmered all this through their thick lips
Plans against Africa while playing with fire
Unaware that anyone who had frizzy hair
Had a duty to protect the continent against blue eyes
Eyes of flames ready to burn our dense forests.

These blacks returning from the west
Were nothing but morons.
Empty like the wind,
They satisfied their gruesome appetites
Without taking into account our children.

We were caught in the crossfire; on one side
The white settlers, and on the other his servants, the corrupted blacks
Who disregarded the words of the giant of humanity
General de Gaulle who spoke: "Countries have no friends
They have only interests."

Some black children arose:
Marien Ngouabi and Patrice Lumumba
Were cowardly assassinated.
So were Thomas Sankara and Kwame Nkrumah
Who knew that independence was not won yet

II

Then Mother Africa closed her eyes. Shamed
By the stupidity of her trapped children. Thoughtful mother!
From blue eyes emanated a certain revenge
We could not understand its origin.
We had been hitherto
Submissive, obedient, even when we should not;
There had been no hypocrisy for centuries
In our behaviour, even when we were chosen
To be beaten with chains or fists.
Like spoiled children who are sent to the corner,
We have been obedient and polite,
Breathing the smell of damp mouldy walls.
In prison, in the holds, and even under water
We stayed calm and said no word
Curled up on ourselves in the marine cold
Mouths closed and keeping our noses open.

Cleansed of all impurities and insults
We suffered in silence without rebelling,
Committing suicide rather than answering evil with evil
Leaving only the guilty to wash his dirty hands.
We received a slap on one cheek
Turning the other we were drawn in the mud.
Our voices as women were raised
Pleading while they raped us: "Pity
Help, help" did we shout
Watching our babies tumbling down staircases.
With these filthy sins
We thought this must be the end of the world.
We opened the eyes with astonishment
Then closed them while waiting for the judgement.
Long wait, an eternity!
Finally independence, thank God, relieved!
But our intellectuals and their education,
Bleached and washed forgot our lamentations.
From Paris, Brussels, Washington, London
They received their masters' orders.
To dominate, conquer, they practiced division.
They all lived night and day in betrayal.
Their politics urged them to kill
If they did not want to be killed;
Politics whose reins were held by those in the west
Who when they saw us united gnashed their teeth.
Having been in their schools and even in their rooms
Our people learned from January 1 to December 31
Their way of speaking and thinking
Their way of singing and dancing
Pursuing their dreams every day and every night
Dreams of grandeur, madness, and even in the rain,
They wanted to see them turn into reality
Even though it pushed them away from the truth.

In suits and ties they harangued the innocent
Crowds caught in a swell
Consisting of mislead people
Heralding words of false promise.
As we savoured these dark sayings,
The eyes of their masters were shining in the shadows
They had placed their lions on us
They handled them like little pawns.
Sitting there in the distance they rubbed their hands
Happy for our people were preparing their tomorrows.
They threw them crumbs for pity
Which made them the nouveau riche in the neighbourhood
While all around them were dying those who
Requested nothing but to live for a grain of rice.

Yes their hat was still in good care
While their flag was already far

This was not a bold stroke
Neither a feat
Even less a coup de grace
But a real coup d'état

Today

One can no longer tell where to turn to
Our eyes remain raised towards the heavens
Our lips refrain from praising
And rising pious hymns to the Saints

After a long life spent in prison
We come out annihilated
Poor in the eyes of God, the king, and the colonizer
Completely inhabited by corrupt memories.

My God, the worst is yet to come! Suffering again
The best is still in pain
Believing in happiness and not dying
Enduring to live until the deliverance

These new black dictators with their distended bellies
Displaying a foreign language and rhetoric
Thunder louder than the speakers
While we expect our daily bread.

For the famine, the disease, these pains
Which are our best companions
Dominate on all the false words
Coming out of the mouths of our boss-brothers.

These intellectuals, fingers of our hand
Whom we venerated even yesterday again
Our only hope, saviours of our tomorrows
We had praised them in vain.

These dictators, all beggars and stupid
Set apart each day into political parties
To live greedy souls
As alcoholics

Tossed left to right by masters
Who have merely changed their suits
Slave traders, missionaries, colonizers, traitors
My God! Our leaders should simply turn back to our customs.

Cause no matter how long the tree
Stays in water they say,
The water will not turn that tree
Into a crocodile

The last word

Here you go, Nandji
That is our story
Our legend
Soon I will join our ancestors
I will tell them that I told you our epic
I will tell them also
What they do not know yet
About the world which is falling apart
Cause since their departure
This world has changed
Who knows…
They might have the answer
Remember
We are griots of mankind
Of truth
Of knowledge
Of wisdom
Tell the story to your children
And when time comes
Come join us
Come tell us what we will not know
Because the world changes every second
And who knows…
Maybe we will have answers

(Tales and legends of MAM'KAYI)

LAST BOOK

Establish for us good laws, equitable laws then we will in return apply a fair trial. But every time you vote laws and texts to suit your whims, just to satisfy your temporary interests, the magistrate will rise. He will teach you to take for the citizens for whom he guarantees freedoms, correct laws, without emotional influence so as to let live forever, the spirit of the state.

Anatole Collinet Makosso, Right of Scrutiny, evidence from a messenger of Congo-Brazzaville

Judgement

Accused! Well, go to the bar
Here we are! The African sun is known to be strong
By itself it takes care of the barbarian
There you are alone, nobody by your side not even the west.

Look before you and listen to the silence
Watch the markets, rivers, and fields
Where are spread the mangled bodies, your audience
Which in the deep night raises its sad song!

Hide yourself and turn a deaf ear
An invisible look keeps on staring at you
Pointing its big toe towards you.
Fifty years of crimes against humanity!

Accused one, stand up! Silence in court!
Look at me. Good! Above the nose!
You are worse than those who locked us in the basement.
Do not look down, lift up your gaze. Accused!

Open your ears, listen to these murmurs
Whispers of children, accusing whispers
Which rise and shout through the walls
"Let justice be done to the criminal!"

Come on, answer, guilty or not guilty?
Widows believe in your guilt
Orphans know what you are capable of
So endorse your liability.

Hell, heat of fire, mister the truth
You will know it and it will set you free.
Therefore the truth and nothing but the truth
Lift up your right hand and say, "I swear!" Go on!

Assert, state, feel the nausea
That arises and conquers your neck
Head, ears, eyes and your throat
You see, isn't it madness, rejoice in all

Theft, murder and rape of a woman
Guilty and capable no confusion
Does her suffering remind you of this infamous offence?
Go, run but vomit, feel the pressure.

You didn't do it, but you liked it, do deny
Slave driver, missionary, settler, dictator, ventriloquist
The hummingbird on top of the tree saw you from its nest
Dragging mother Africa like a rag.

She was bleeding in front of you, stretching out her entrails
Innocent, harmless, distracted…
Arms up you were leading the battle
And she crouched, twisted

In your follies, joys and angers
You stabbed her with a thousand and one knives.
The water of African rivers originally clear
Became red blood of your crime, bad torturer

Painful death, the pain is dead
Finally satisfied? What future
Do you leave in front of the door
So heaven may bless you?

The world is not fooled; it supports the sentence
Observe the lines of your hand, do you see that blood
Flowing through your veins?
The world is not fooled; it is watching you, suspicious

Defendant! Respond, unburden yourself, do it!
And rush towards life, progress
Stop acting as a greedy man
For money, wealth, for…express your regrets

It's so awful isn't it, being covered
With shame, dishonour; but the truth
Like a tree with green foliage
Will take care of you, and the griot will exclaim: "What humility!"

Believe me this is not a poem
It is the voice of conscience that comes to your rescue
It is the work of man no one has chosen it
Defendant, answer and stop playing deaf

The griot will go from village to village
He will comfort consciences and souls.
It is the work of man he will go from shore to shore
Comforting children and women

All will sing a jubilant Africa
Without tears, without mourning
A melody of a new wisdom
Coming right from the heart

And the sky will open! Wonder!
Like a flower that awakens!
Forever!
For love!

The verdict

Murmurs and buzzing

- The court
- We sit down
- Quiet!
Blow of a hammer
- Did you read the verdict?
-Yes, your honour
'To the question:
Is the accused guilty and responsible for 50 years of crimes against humanity?
The jury responded:
Yes, guilty!'

Murmurs and buzzing
A blow of a hammer

- Court is adjourned

The dying one
by Naolicha Li Maxy, Law school graduate

I stand in front of him
He's lying on a bed
In a hospital
Dying
Cancer of power
His face is serene
But his eyes betray a deep bitterness.

I blame him for having remorse
On his deathbed
All the battles he fought
With no importance
All these betrayals just for a piece of bread
Didn't he see that during each of his wars,
He was losing a part of his body?

Today his limbs are of no use to him.
He has ears
That cannot hear
A mouth that cannot talk
His punishment is to see the human work he has done

Nothing doctors can do now
He is involved in activities that are harmful to him.
He does not even bother
Reading the prescriptions handed to him.
It would have been better for him to stay slave
Even his masters would not allow him to destroy himself that way

Nobody at his bedside
Not even that master with whom
He shared a glass of champagne
Or that friend with whom he fought beside

Nobody
It's only me
Moreover, I have always been here
But in his eyes I did not exist
Did he once address me by my mother or my daughter?

I could not contain my tears
How could a man have
So little regard for his own person
Only fifty years and he was dying

He holds out his hand
His eyes beg me to take it
While I lay my hand in his
I see his eyes close
A smile appears on his face.
He's gone
The father of the nation is dead
From a cancer
The cancer of power
Peace to his soul.

APPENDICE

The planet is only a village,
It is so easy to speak the same language
(Alpha Blondy)

MOTHER AFRICA,

YOUR INDEPENDENCE IS STILL A LONG WAY TO GO
YOUR FREEDOM IS STILL FAR AWAY
AS FOR DEMOCRACY
-DEMOCRACY? WHAT AGAIN DOES THAT
STRANGE WORD STAND FOR?
-IS IT AN AFRICAN WORD?
-NO, I DON'T THINK SO.

Listen Africa what your leaders said :

President-poet Leopold Sedar Senghor (October 9, 1906 – December 20, 2001)

> *"I think that in an underdeveloped country the best thing to have is but a single party, at least a unified party, a dominant party where the contradictions of reality merge between them within the dominant party on the understanding that it is the party that handles them and decides."*

In August 1960 Senegal obtains independence and in September Senghor is voted in as its president. He will hold office until December 31, 1980 when he resigns of his own will in favour of Abdou Diouf, whom he had chosen as his successor and prepared to hold office.

President Felix Houphouët Boigny (Octobre 18, 1905 – December 7, 1993)

> *"We are only newly born to independent living. We have inherited from French people not a nation but a state. The nation is a construction that follows a permanent effort. Everywhere multiparty system has been instituted, tribal feuds were revived. We must rise above tribal feuds. In Ivory Coast as in most African countries, multiparty system does not help unity."*

Houphouët- Boigny became prime minister of Côte d'Ivoire (Ivory Coast) in 1959 and was elected the first president of the independent country in 1960. Affectionately called "Papa Houphouët" or "le vieux" he was president from independence in 1960 until his death in 1993.

President Sekou Toure (January 9, 1922 – March 26, 1984)

> *"The State party of Guinea in its ideology that is already developed, has defined the category it refers to as class people that constitutes its social base and whose components have a common interest in its struggle. The class people in a revolutionary regime, has therefore all the power and authority to preserve and strengthen social justice forever. It becomes clear that the individuals or groups of individuals with interests opposed to that historical view are not part of the class people."*

Sekou Toure was an African political leader and president of Guinea from independence in 1958 to his death in 1984.

President Mobutu Sese Seko (October 14, 1930 – September 7, 1997)

> *"Citizens, Activists campaigners,*
> *Liberal democracy, popular democracy, parliamentary system, left-wing party, right wing party, extreme left party, extreme right party, centre left party, centre right party, centre party in a word, flexible bipartisanship, rigid two-party system, we have nothing to envy from all these regimes that have instituted multiparty systems in their home with a variety of opposition parties.*
> *And in my lifetime, a two-party, or multiparty systems in Zaire, this will never happen. It is quite clear."*

Mobutu was the president of Zaire (now called the Democratic Republic of Congo, independent since June 1960) for much of his reign from 1965 to 1997.

President Omar Bongo (December 30, 1935 – June 8, 2009)

> *"I tell you and I even can confirm it: the multiparty system in Gabon, 'nought' and while I am here, there will be none of it."*

Omar Bongo was president of Gabon (independent since 1960) for 42 years from 1967 until his death in office, in 2009.

Then, having thought about it, the president-poet Senghor who remembers once having said:

> *The farmer will speak*
> *The worker will discuss*
> *The intellectual will talk*
> *The politician will express his view*
> *Women will talk..."* becomes the poet-president then he switches sides. He steps down before the power leaves him, to the disappointment of other African leaders, then proclaims:

"Dear Mr. First president,
After having seriously considered the situation, I have decided to resign from my position as president of the Republic. The Supreme Court is the vigilant guardian of our constitution. That is why I have the honour, Mr. first president, to hand in my resignation into your hands.
I beg you, under the constitution to draw the consequences and to agree with the sermon by Mr. Abdou Diouf[10] *the current prime minister, who is to replace me.*
In advance, please be thanked."

THE POET-PRESIDENT
LEOPOLD SEDAR SENGHOR

♦♦♦

Children feel no hatred or vengeance
They know neither honour nor glory; bad luck,
Faithful throughout their journey
Settles down wickedly, quietly among them.
Today they are their own parents, tomorrow
Their fate will be decided in their own hands.
No man, no god will turn to them
Unless the man created in God's image
Man, the very man with a human heart,
Not the religious, not the politician
Rather the poet, the righteous one, and not the emotionless heart,
But the man of love who is still alive on earth
Pushes away from them starvation and disease

---

[10] Abdou Diouf (born September 7, 1935), former president of the Republic of Senegal (1981-2000), was elected secretary General of the Francophonie Summit in Beirut in 2002. Took office in 2003, was re-elected first in 2006 by the Heads of State and government at the Bucharest Summit, and again in 2010 at the Summit of Montreux.
Abdou Diouf has fought for greater African Unity, including assuming the duties of chairman of the Organisation of African Unity (OAU, July 1985-July 1986 then in 1992) and chairman of the Economic Community of West African States (ECOWAS, July 1991-July 1992)

Civil wars and guns
Unless the woman, the righteous, the true one, faith-filled
Even in her labour pains rises and cries out loud
"Enough!
Stop!"
While the drilled bodies still litter the earth,
And the echo commands weapons to keep quiet
"Stop in the name of God!
Cease fire!"

♦♦♦

Fear God and keep his commandments, because this applies to every person. For God will bring every work into judgement, including every secret thing, whether good or evil.
ECCLESIASTE 12 :13-14

Execute true justice, show mercy and compassion everyone to his brother. Do not oppress the widow or the orphan, the stranger or the poor. Let none of you plan evil in his heart against his brother.
ZECHARIAH 7 : 9-10

Notes about Pan-Africanists

Marien Ngouabi (December 31, 1938 – March 18, 1977) was the military president of the Republic of Congo Brazzaville from January 1, 1969 until his death in 1977. He was assassinated by an alleged suicide commando. After 70 years of French colonisation, the Republic of Congo became independent in August 15, 1960.

> *"When your country is dirty and lacks lasting peace, you can restore its cleanliness and its unity by washing it with your blood."*
> Marien Ngouabi, March 13, 1977, last speech at the City Hall place in Brazzaville

Patrice Lumumba (July 2, 1925 - January 17, 1961) was a Congolese independence leader and the first legally elected prime minister of the Republic Democratic of Congo after he helped with its independence from Belgium in June 1960. Only 10 weeks later Lumumba's government was deposed in a coup during the Congo crisis. He was subsequently imprisoned and murdered.

> *"Don't weep my love, one day history will have its say. Not the history they teach in Brussels, Paris or Washington, but our History. That of new Africa, the newborn Africa."* Patrice Lumumba

Kuamé Nkrumah (21 September, 1909 – 27 April, 1972) is a Ghanaian nationalist leader who led the Gold Coast's drive for independence from Britain and presided over its emergence as the new nation of Ghana. He headed the country from independence in March 6, 1957 until he was overthrown by a coup in 1966. He's the father of Pan-Africanisme. He wanted a united Africa where the raw materials would be used not only for the development of Europe but also would greatly contribute to making Africa a major economic power.

> *"Africa is a paradox which illustrates and highlights neo-colonialism. Her earth is rich, yet the products that come from above and below the soil continue to enrich, not Africans predominantly, but groups and individuals who operate to Africa's impoverishment."* Kwamé Nkrumah

Thomas Sankara (21 December, 1949 – 15 October, 1987) was the president and head of state of Burkina Faso from August 4, 1983 to October 1987. He was 37 years and 10 months old when he was assassinated. Called the President of the people, Thomas Sankara was a man of integrity and a visionary leader. Fighting against all forms of oppression and injustice, his influence persists in Africa and around the world. He wanted simply to see Africa looking up, an Africa proud and recognized at fair value.

He changed the name of his country formerly called Upper Volta, a name inherited from the colonial period, to Burkina Faso, which in the African tradition means, "Land of honest men." This politician and Pan-Africanist revolutionary bequeathed to Africa a major political heritage and identity. Because of his work and personality, Thomas Sankara was, and remains a great role model for African youth.

> *"The greatest difficulty consists in the spirit of neo-colonizing we have in this country. We were colonized by France, which gave us some habits. For us to succeed in life, to have happiness is to try to live as in France, as the richest of the French. So that is why the changes we want to make face obstacles and fall." Thomas Sankara*

♦♦♦

"Africa and the world are yet to recover from Sankara's assassination. Just as we have yet to recover from the loss of Patrice Lumumba, Kuamé Nkrumah, Eduardo Mondlane, *Mozambique (20 June, 1920-3 February, 1969)*, Amilcar Cabral, *Guinea-Bissau (12 September, 1924 - 20 January, 1973)*, Steve Biko, *South Africa (18 December, 1946 - 12 September, 1977)*, Samora Machel, *Mozambique (29 September, 1933 - 19 October, 1986)*, and most recently John Garang, *Sudan (23 June 1945 - 30 July 2005)* to name only a few. While malevolent forces have not used the same methods to eliminate each of these great Pan-Africanists, they have been guided by the same motive: to keep Africa in chains."

Antonio de Figueiredo, journalist and writer from Portugal (18 March, 1929 - 30 November, 2006)

A note on the translator

Originally from Congo Brazzaville, Michel Poati-Tchicaya holds a Master Degree in Linguistics and English language then a post Master Degree Diploma in Psycho-mechanics of Modern Languages. Based in London with his family, Michel has been an administrator, a translator and English lecturer in a London private college then a Lecturer of French for British Adults in a local college. In charge of the proofreading of a French newspaper based in London, he also takes part to its texts writing for the paper. Michel specialized himself in Interpreting and Translation as well as devoting his spare time to writing and now publishing his works.

Special thanks to my English proofreaders:

Elena Rogers
Jan De Grass
Tanya Evanson
Teoni Spathelfer
Elisha Starbright

And also to

Joanna Mackenzie and Bjorn Enga
Judith Mathieu
Melanie Ray
Bonnie Hutchinson
David Kipling
Kathy Vance

In homage to my mother Ma M'kayi
Born MARIE-THERESE MAKAYA, alias SYLVIE
Who spent her life telling me
Wonderful stories
And who unfortunately leaves me
At the age of seventy five
Taken by a heart attack
This Tuesday November 1st 2011
On my birthday
At the time that I am about to send
Human Works
To my editor

« Dear mother, your spirit is born just on the same day you gave birth to me. I cried when from Paris your granddaughter Prisca phoned me in vancouver to tell me the sad news. All together, holding the phone in one hand, wiping tears with the other hand, we cried for about an hour. Sitting in my car I wept like a kid…your kid. I cried the entire day and the entire night from the first to the second of November. At the gleam of fall, I realized that you will always remain in my heart… You will live forever. You just wanted some rest and went away…

I love you.

This book is dedicated to you. It is the fruit of your teachings; teachings that my five brothers: Auguste, Michel, Anatole, Celestin, Christian Cesar and myself who are still on this side, and our two sisters Bernadette and Brigitte Flore who, I am certain are in the Lord`s peace, and who welcome you joyfully on the other side over there I hope, all benefited.

Because of you, we went to a good school. Your school. The one that I like to call 'MA M'KAYI'S SCHOOL'.

I will never forget you though I can't be there to say good bye. I would've loved to be there, believe me. I would've paid the price just to be there, the same price you paid for me to become the man I am today. Yes I would've paid it…just to be there ! But when you're a 'national mother', your funeral becomes state funeral. Indeed, you were the mother of the whole nation. Even the first lady, Antoinette - muane Nguli, daughter of your tribe, and members of the gorvenment were there to offer you their respects. Ma M'Kayi, you were a great soul and a great heart.

I am infinetely thankful that I inherited your storytelling skills, an art so valued by your ancestors.
Your teaching Marie-Therese is a diamond ornament around my neck. Thank you !

MUANAKU
Your child

One more thing... I know you'll be fine. You will remain exactly the same in my heart and my mind, for ever. You were not ill or in distress...That's the way I will always remember you...you were always strong and full of life...
Joyful and...when I think about your contagious smile I...well...

Take care you, woman of the fields, woman of great things !
Keep smiling !
See you soon !

Table of Contents

Acknowledgements 5
Introduction 7
Preface 11

BOOK ONE 13
    Orphans 15
    Ascension 19
    Faith and hope 20
    Mutual transition 25
    Smile and memory 27
    Homeless 28

BOOK II 31
    Nandji or she 33
    Nandji Iya Navandji or she and the other 34
    The tale of Ma M'kayi 36

BOOK III 39
    The history 41
    Abundance 42
    Stampede 44
    The black king and the white master 45
        The white master 46
        The black king 47
    Sale 49

BOOK IV 51
    Mission and vision 53
    Foreigners I 55
    The sacred book 55
    Foreigners II 56
    Hell and Heaven 57
    Preaching 58
    Baptism 59
    Currency of Judas 60

BOOK V 61
    The black king in white boots 63
    The new chief 64
    A king's act 65
    The big speech 66
    Death of the king 67
    With no reply 68

BOOK VI 69
    The colonized ones 71
    Present! Absent! 73
    Letters and numbers 74
    False hope 75

BOOK VII 77
    Song of the griot 79
    Independence (1960) 81

BOOK VIII 83
    The flag and the hat (1960-2010) 85
    Today 89
    The last word 91

LAST BOOK 93
    Judgement 95
    The verdict 98
    The dying one 99

APPENDICE 101
    Listen Africa what your leaders said : 103

Notes about Pan-Africanists 107

A note on the translator 109

In homage to my mother Ma M'kayi 110

www.ingramcontent.com/pod-product-compliance
Lightning Source LLC
Chambersburg PA
CBHW060502110426
42738CB00055B/2456